Joint Center for Political
   Studies (U.S.). Committee
   on Policy for Racial
   Justice.

Visions of a better way.

157864

Visions Of
A Better Way

Visions Of A Better Way

A Black Appraisal Of Public Schooling

Preface by
John Hope Franklin

Joint Center for Political Studies Press
Washington, D.C.
1989

The Joint Center for Political Studies is a national
nonprofit institution that conducts research on public
policy issues of special concern to black Americans
and promotes informed and effective involvement of
blacks in the governmental process. Founded in
1970, the Joint Center provides independent and
nonpartisan analyses through research, publication,
and outreach programs.

Opinions expressed in Joint Center publications are
those of the authors and do not necessarily reflect the
views of the other staff, officers, or governors of the
Joint Center or of the organizations supporting the
Center and its research.

We gratefully acknowledge the Ford Foundation and
the John D. and Catherine T. MacArthur Foundation
for their support of the work of the Committee on
Policy for Racial Justice.

Distributed by arrangement with
University Press of America, Inc.
4720 Boston Way
Lanham, MD 20706

3 Henrietta Street
London WC2E 8LU England

Printed in the United States of America

ISBN 0–941410–76–5

Contents

The Committee on Policy for Racial Justice: Mission and Objectives

The Committee on Policy for Racial Justice conducts independent intellectual inquiry in search of solutions to problems confronting black Americans. In that search the committee members rely on the sage observations made by wise and courageous black spokesmen who have preceded them. One was Frederick Douglass who said, more than a century ago, "If we are ever elevated, our elevation will have been accomplished through our own instrumentality. . . . No People that has solely depended upon [outside] . . . aid . . . ever stood forth in the attitude of Freedom."

Another was William E. B. Du Bois who declared, more than a half century ago, that the progress and ultimate positive resolution of the struggle for racial justice in the United States would depend on the contributions of blacks themselves, who would use their knowledge and skills—in economics, in social policy, in public administration, and in political theory and practice—as weapons in the ongoing struggle for social justice.

The third trenchant observation was made by a great modern leader, Martin Luther King, Jr., who said, "It is not a sign of weakness, but a sign of high maturity to rise to the level of self-criticism . . . [which means] critical thinking about ourselves as a people and the course we have charted or failed to chart during this period."

In this spirit, the Committee meets periodically to review the condition of blacks in American society, to inform itself and others about progress and failures in the struggle for racial equality, and to seek to chart a course that will advance the cause of justice for all.

Foreword

Seven years ago, the Joint Center's Committee on Policy for Racial Justice held its first meeting at Tarrytown, New York, to reflect on the condition of blacks in American society. Since that time, this unique group of black scholars has convened eleven meetings and produced two essays—*A Policy Framework for Racial Justice,* which delineated areas of urgent concern for the black community, and *Black Initiative and Governmental Responsibility,* an examination of the often complicated relationship between blacks and the federal government.

The second of these essays—published by the Joint Center in 1987—received considerable public attention. "The report of these scholars," wrote *Washington Post* columnist David Broder, "is a major contribution to framing a debate on the black community's needs, and can return those issues to the place they deserve on the national agenda."

We issue this third essay, *Visions Of A Better Way: A Black Appraisal Of Public Schooling,* at a time when education has become a major concern of the American people. We hope that national, state, and local governments, as well as corporations and others interested in raising educational standards and enhancing educational equity, will find this a useful document.

The Joint Center is indebted to the members of the Committee for their contributions to the publication of this essay, to Catherine Iino for her editing, and to Constance Toliver for styling the document.

Eddie N. Williams
President
Joint Center for Political Studies

Preface

Of all the problems confronting the black community today, none are more critical to its future than those related to education. The "interlocking effects of deprivation," a phrase used by President Lyndon Johnson in 1965, will not be resolved unless the black community commits itself *en masse* to a dramatic improvement in the quality of public education available to its children. Economic and social progress in the United States has long been rooted in access to quality education. What worked so well for millions of immigrants must at last be made to work for black Americans.

It is this subject which we address in our essay, the third in a series of occasional papers that seek to explore new avenues for improving the lives of black Americans. Much has been written on education by experts and commentators, based on research, observation, opinion polls, interviews, and analyses, and yet our public school system continues to fail large segments of our population. This is not because as a society we are ignorant of what needs to be done or even how to do it, but because for one reason or another we have not been willing to attach the highest priority to education. Unless we do so, millions of black youngsters will remain deprived of the skills they need to function successfully in today's environment.

One of the most thoughtful and distinguished scholars working in this field is Dr. Sara Lawrence Lightfoot, professor of education at Harvard University and a member of the Committee on Policy for Racial Justice. We are fortunate indeed that she was willing to provide the leadership and expertise required to conceptualize and write this essay. With the collaboration of her colleague, Dr. Michael Fultz, she prepared the original document for discussion by the Committee and then skillfully meshed the views and ideas of the members into a coherent whole.

Our essay challenges the excuses made by those who try to rationalize or justify the failures of a public school system which prides itself on being an important vehicle for upward mobility within society and on being the foundation of American democracy. We do not accept any of the facile arguments that seek to evade responsibility for the chronic inequality in our system of education. Second-class schooling for black students, based frequently on low teacher expectations, remains the norm in far too many schools. This phenomenon as well as other barriers to educational achievement are examined in detail in our essay.

In looking at problems facing black students, we intended not only to identify and define these problems but also to search for models of success—schools that are able to educate the much broader, more heterogeneous student population now enrolled in our public schools. We found that such institutions do exist and that one of their common characteristics is a school environment in which students, parents, teachers, principals, and the community are active participants.

Significant changes are taking place in school systems around the country. More and more urban schools have become predominantly black in the composition of the student body, teaching staff, and administrators. Roughly 1,580 blacks currently serve as school board members and more than 125 as school superintendents. Accession to office by blacks, however, in no way guarantees that they will be able to bring about significant changes quickly or easily, since political power and economic resources frequently remain firmly rooted in the old, mainly white power structure. But the black community must insist on educational excellence for its children, regardless of who is in charge of the system.

Demographic realities point toward a work force that by the year 2000 will look very different from today's. For economic reasons, if no other, this society will have to pay far greater attention to the ethnic and cultural diversity of students currently enrolled in our public schools and provide them with the tools they need to become productive citizens. It is encouraging to know that the black community's concern about the education of its children is shared by at least some of America's most influential political, corporate, and industrial leaders.

This essay should make it clear that we expect to be active participants in the accelerating national debate on the future of public education. We are eager to share our recommendations for reforms with other concerned individuals, particularly black leaders. We identify three interconnected areas in which progressive educational reform can be achieved:

- recognizing the centrality of human relationships;
- eliminating barriers to effective teaching and learning;
- mobilizing physical and political resources.

But the bottom line is that schools must assume the responsibility of educating all children, regardless of racial, ethnic, social, or economic background.

We hope you will find this essay a useful and persuasive document and will share our determination to pursue a radical improvement in the quality of American public education.

John Hope Franklin
April 1989

How many effective schools would you have to see to be persuaded of the educability of poor children? If your answer is more than one, then I suspect that you have reasons of your own for preferring to believe that basic pupil performance derives from family background instead of the school's response to family background.

—Ronald Edmonds, 1979

Introduction

We hold this truth to be self-evident: *all black children are capable of learning and achieving.* Others who have hesitated, equivocated, or denied this fact have assumed that black children could not master their schoolwork or have cautioned that blacks were not "academically oriented." As a result, they have perpetuated a myth of intellectual inferiority, perhaps genetically based. These falsehoods prop up an inequitable social hierarchy with blacks disproportionately represented at the bottom, and they absolve schools of their fundamental responsibility to educate all children, no matter how deprived.

Affirming the intellectual capability of black youth is a political act, because the promise of equal opportunity and participatory democracy in the United States depends on an egalitarian view of human potential. Issues of black academic ability, social justice, and community empowerment are thus inextricably linked. Activism on behalf of better public education can provide a sense of purpose for black communities throughout the nation.

And what we must demand is this: that the schools shift their focus from the supposed deficiencies of the black child—from the alleged inadequacies of black family life—to the barriers that stand in the way of academic success. Since the concept of the "culturally deprived child" emerged in the early 1960s, far too much attention has been paid to the character-

1

What we must demand is this: that the schools shift their focus from the supposed deficiencies of the black child—from the alleged inadequacies of black family life—to the barriers that stand in the way of academic success.

istics of black youth, particularly their deviations from mainstream norms, rather than to the structural mechanisms through which schools replicate the divisions of the broader society.[1] We do not discount the effects of poverty, racism, and segregation on individuals. Societal hostility and neglect have taken a tremendous toll upon our people; many of us have internalized social pressures as self-doubt or even in pathological responses, as scholars E. Franklin Frazier and Kenneth Clark and writers Richard Wright, Lorraine Hansberry, and James Baldwin have vividly shown.[2] Yet scattered examples of effective schooling for poor and minority children, a few—often unheralded—intervention models, and countless instances of individual accomplishments convince us that the essential problem lies not with the academic potential of black children but with the unproductive institutional arrangements, lowered expectations, and narrow pedagogical processes that characterize the American educational system.[3]

The late Ron Edmonds, a leader of the effective schools movement, wrote in 1979, "Repudiation of the social science notion that family background is the principal cause of pupil acquisition of basic school skills is probably a prerequisite to successful reform of public schooling for children of the poor."[4] We heartily concur. Black families, like all others, exert a critical influence on the development of their children's character, personalities, and general orientation to life and learning. But the promise of American education is to take children as it finds them and educate them. It is the school's responsibility to overcome those social barriers that limit academic progress.

American schooling in general has again become a topic of hot debate and intense criticism. American children are lagging behind children of other countries in academic achievement, at a time when higher and higher levels of skills are needed for national economic advancement. In the new, post-industrial, service and information society, achieving productive employment, performing contemporary tasks, and making informed social, economic, and political decisions depend more than ever on the highest levels of educational attainment.

At the same time, schools are being asked to educate a much broader, more heterogeneous student population than ever before. While we acknowledge this burden on resources and creativity, we also believe that the conspicuous failure of many urban public school systems to adapt to the changing nature of society, coupled with their traditional disregard for the needs and abilities of those not considered to be in the mainstream (because of race, gender, or class), amounts to educational disfranchisement.[5]

This essay focuses on public schools, not independent or parochial schools, because the vast majority of black children attend public institutions and because it is with regard to public schools that the national agenda on education is fashioned. To be sure, some working-class and middle-class black families have abandoned the public schools. We believe, however, that most have done so reluctantly, and at great financial hardship, aware that they are losing a sense of community but hoping to find individual attention and more creative pedagogical approaches in private schools.

We center our comments on children and adolescents, particularly those deemed "at risk" or "educationally disadvantaged," because this period in life is educationally and developmentally crucial for all youngsters. We do not discuss the problems of higher education for blacks, the declines in student aid, the retreat from affirmative action, or the abuse of black student athletes. Nor do we discuss the role of black colleges, with their special strengths and vulnerabilities. These are all critical issues for the black community to consider, but they are beyond the purview of this essay.

One major theme this framework *does* emphasize, which recent reports have largely ignored, is the centrality of *human relationships* in education. Testing and tracking are obvious topics of discussion; the lack of reinforcing relationships in the learning experiences of black children is equally at issue.[6] Neither teaching nor learning is a purely mechanical process. Few children are motivated to inquire into the wonders of the world around them if they are not aided by a warm and caring relationship with another human being. Studies show, for example, that the

The promise of American education is to take children as it finds them and educate them. It is the school's responsibility to overcome those social barriers that limit academic progress.

3

educational mission of the television program *Sesame Street* is more effective with middle-class children than with poor children because it is frequently interpreted to them by a primary care giver.[7] In many—though by no means all—low-income families, parents and guardians do not have the time, the energy, or the skills to reinforce the informal learning opportunities that might take place in the home or in local facilities.

We applaud the resurgence of concern about the state of American education in general. Certain aspects of the current educational reform movement, however, are troubling and potentially divisive. For example, higher standards are a laudable goal, but within the present context supportive structures must be created, and sufficient funds must be allocated, to ensure that those who have had difficulties in the past will be able to meet the new requirements. To sing a psalm of excellence while failing to attend to the plight of underachievers is to make a mockery of the goal of school improvement for all. Likewise, to blame the idealism of the 1960s for the current problems in American education while cutting funds for programs assisting poor and disadvantaged students—as the Reagan administration did—is to debase the widespread impulse for social justice among the American people.[8] Educational reform must respond to the concerns of all constituents; schooling in a democratic society must embrace the least privileged as well as those who come to the classroom better prepared.

Edmonds once noted that "schools teach those they think they must and when they think they needn't they don't." The black community must demand that its children receive the proper instruction and necessary resources to fulfill their potential.

One major theme this framework does emphasize, which recent reports have largely ignored, is the centrality of human relationships in education.

4

*The caste spirit is rampant in the land; it is laying
hold of the public schools and it has the colored
public schools by the throat, North, East, South, and
West. Beware of it, my brothers and dark sisters;
educate your children. Give them the broadest and
highest education possible; train them to the limit of
their ability, if you work your fingers to the bone
doing it. . . . Never forget that if we ever compel the
world's respect, it will be by virtue of our heads, and
not our heels.*

—W. E. B. Du Bois, 1912

The Historical Context

In 1934, the black educator Horace Mann Bond, later
to be the first black president of Lincoln University
in Pennsylvania and the father of civil rights activist
Julian Bond, published a classic study in black
educational history, *The Education of the Negro in
the American Social Order.* In this highly acclaimed,
meticulously researched volume, Bond carefully
traces the black community's efforts to achieve
educational advancement. It is a tale of heroic
accomplishments in the face of persistent discrimination and denial. As important, though, Bond bril-
liantly reveals the essential tensions in the black
community's historical relationship to schooling.
On the one hand, black Americans, like whites, have
firmly believed in education's role "as the most
important factor in elevating the life of a people"—
indeed, Bond believed that schooling should function
to "accelerate social change." On the other hand,
Bond recognized the school's inextricable links to the
political and economic structures of society and thus
to the *status quo.* "Strictly speaking," he wrote, "the
school has never built a new social order; it has
been the product and interpreter of the existing
system, sustaining and being sustained by the
social complex."[9]

Many others, of course, have noted the tension between hope and frustration in the black experience with public education—the contrast between blacks' passionate belief in the democratic principles of equal rights and opportunities and the reality of prejudice and discrimination in and out of school. As early as 1819, the valedictorian of an African Free School in New York remarked:

> Why should I strive hard and acquire all the constituents of a man, if the prevailing genius of the land admit me not as such or but in an inferior degree! Pardon me if I feel insignificant and weak. . . . What are my prospects? To what shall I turn my hand? Shall I be a mechanic? No one will employ me; white boys won't work with me. Shall I be a merchant? No one will have me in his office; white clerks won't associate with me. Drudgery and serviture, then, are my prospective portion. Can you be surprised at my discouragement?[10]

Many have noted the contrast between blacks' passionate belief in the democratic principles of equal rights and opportunities and the reality of prejudice and discrimination in and out of school.

Succeeding generations of black students have experienced similar conditions and have reiterated these sentiments tenfold.

The history of the black community's relationship to schooling is, we believe, critical to a consideration of the contemporary scene, because as in other areas the problems our people face today have often been foreshadowed in the past. We are interested in retrieving the essence of historical lessons that allowed black people to surmount some extraordinary obstacles, lessons which reveal our strengths and our frustrations in the ongoing climb, as Dr. King put it, toward the mountaintop.

The desire to learn to read and to write was keen in the black communities of antebellum America, both among the free Negro population in the North and in the slave culture of the South. Even in the dilapidated log cabins of the slave quarters the desire for education was nurtured and strengthened as an integral part of the socialization patterns and kinship networks of black men and women held in bondage.[11]

For most of the eighteenth century and until the second decade of the nineteenth century, the education of the slave population, while never extensive, proceeded as a matter of economic necessity. Slaves were trained as skilled artisans—carpenters, mechanics, draftsmen, and so on—in order for the plantation to run as an economically efficient unit. In addition, many slave owners taught Bible-reading—stressing, to be sure, those passages that taught obedience to one's master. All this changed, however, when cotton production soared during the first third of the nineteenth century and as slave insurrections and the abolitionist movement gathered momentum. Between 1817 and 1835, a wave of repressive legislation swept the South, prohibiting the assembly of slaves without the presence of whites and strictly enforcing anti-education edicts. One member of the Virginia House of Delegates commented, "We have as far as possible closed every avenue by which light may enter [the slaves'] minds. If we could extinguish the capacity to see the light, our work would be completed; they would then be on a level with the beasts of the field and we would be safe!" Although the slaves themselves continued to strive for knowledge, these laws were rigidly enforced. Thus, by the Civil War, only an estimated five percent of the South's four million slaves were literate.[12]

In the antebellum North, the life of free blacks was severely circumscribed by racism and discriminatory employment practices. (After 1800, it was not uncommon for European observers to remark that racial animosity was strongest in those states which had abolished slavery.) Educational facilities were generally provided for black children—the African Free Schools in New York were exemplary—but typically under segregated conditions, with fewer materials and often hostile white instructors. In Providence, Rhode Island, for example, an early eighteenth century teacher threatened his black students with punishment if they dared to greet him in public.[13]

After the 1820s, northern black communities began a concerted drive for integrated facilities. Although some black parents felt that strengthening the segregated schools would heighten achievement (their children would not be subjected to racial taunts in all-black institutions, and black teachers might find employment), most believed that racial coeducation would begin to break down the barriers of prejudice and would improve classroom resources. Yet white

The desire to learn to read and to write was keen in the black communities of antebellum America, both among the free Negro population in the North and in the slave culture of the South.

7

leaders of the common school movement, such as the legendary Horace Mann, remained ambivalent to the idea of integrated education, and most northern cities and towns were vociferously hostile. The townspeople of Canaan, New Hampshire, for example, were so opposed to Noyes Academy when it opened as an integrated facility in 1835 that they gathered all of the available oxen, tied ropes around the school, and, to wild cheering, literally tore the institution off its foundation. In Canterbury, Connecticut, before the Civil War, abolitionist Prudence Crandell was jailed for her attempt to start an integrated boarding school for girls. "Open this door," the town's elected officials cried, "and New England will become the Liberia of America." In Boston, a black parent, Benjamin Roberts, sued the city in 1849 because his five-year-old daughter, Sarah, had to pass five white schools on her way to the colored primary school. The Massachusetts Supreme Court ultimately ruled against Roberts, upholding the regulatory powers of the city's Primary School Committee and thus establishing a legal precedent for separate but equal education.[14] (Note, however, that in 1855 the Massachusetts legislature prohibited segregated schools throughout the state.)

During and immediately after the Civil War, the black quest for education burst forth. "Free, then, with a desire for land and a frenzy for schools, the Negro lurched into a new day," W. E. B. Du Bois remarked. Booker T. Washington's first-hand impressions were equally vivid: "Few people who were not right in the midst of the scenes can form any exact idea of the intense desire which the people of my race showed for an education. . . . it was a whole race trying to go to school. Few were too young, and none too old, to make the attempt to learn. . . . Day-school, night-school, Sunday-school, were always crowded, and often many had to be turned away for want of room."[15]

*A*fter the 1820s, northern black communities began a concerted drive for integrated facilities.

The Reconstruction governments of the former rebel states, pushed especially by black delegates to the constitutional conventions, established free public school systems in the South. The question of segregated versus multiracial education was generally decided in favor of the former. Rather than threaten the fragile educational systems developing in the late

1860s and early 1870s, black political leaders tended to opt for the best educational facilities possible, however racially populated. As Bond astutely observed:

> Those who argued against mixed schools were right in believing that such a system was impossible for the South, but they were wrong in believing that the South could, or would, maintain equal schools for both races. Those who argued for mixed schools were right in believing that separate schools meant discrimination against Negroes, but they were opposed to the logic of history and the reality of human nature and racial prejudices.[16]

The 50-year period from 1880 to 1930 looms large in black educational history. During this period, black schooling in the South was brought almost to a halt through underfunding and neglect; the Washington-Du Bois debate over industrial versus higher education reached a fevered pitch; intelligence testing became a popular tool to reinforce notions of white genetic intellectual superiority; and patterns of de facto school segregation in the North became firmly established. Although this period has been called the Progressive Era, for the black community the proliferation of lynchings, the exploitation of share-crop tenant farmers, the rise of "Jim Crow" racism, and the widespread acceptance of separate and unequal education forecast a seemingly endless descent, characterized by historian Rayford Logan as "the nadir."[17]

In the South, the 1880s and 1890s saw the rise to political power of demagogues such as Governor James K. Vardaman in Mississippi and Senator "Pitchfork" Ben Tillman in South Carolina, who symbolized an unleashing of perhaps the most virulent forms of racism this nation has experienced. Although proposals to divide school funds according to taxes paid by race or to close down completely all "colored" schools were never enacted into law, Southern and border states systematically proceeded to adopt rigid segregation laws, to disfranchise black voters, and to divert funding for black education to separate schools for whites. The federal government acquiesced, and northern newspapers and academicians condemned black efforts for equality during Reconstruction as graft-ridden folly.[18]

Du Bois and Washington, each in his own way, promoted black schooling during a period when other, stronger forces sought to curtail black intellectual growth.

9

Such was the situation in 1900 when Booker T. Washington and W. E. B. Du Bois argued over the proper course for black political and social development. It is futile to debate the question of who "won" this historic confrontation. Black participation in higher education, which Du Bois eloquently supported, has been an essential component in the twentieth-century civil rights movement, while the need to establish an economic foundation through industrial education and black businesses, which Washington articulated, is still a central problem for black communities throughout the nation. Often overlooked in the commentary on their confrontation is the fact that both men fervently believed in the critical role education must play for blacks to overcome the prevailing discrimination of the nation and achieve the respect due all people. Du Bois and Washington, each in his own way, promoted black schooling during a period when other, stronger forces sought to curtail black intellectual growth.[19]

From the 1930s to the early 1960s, when the civil rights movement blossomed, the central story in black educational history is the legal strategy that culminated in the Brown *decision.*

The other central features of this period, intelligence testing and segregated schooling in the North, often went hand in hand. Following World War I and the first "Great Migration" of blacks to the North, urban black communities in the 1920s grew and consolidated. Restrictive covenants forced blacks to live in burgeoning ghettos, and school district boundaries were drawn to separate black children from their white counterparts. The new fad of mental testing accelerated this push for segregation by reinforcing prejudices and by confusing native intelligence with disparities in environmental conditions.

Did black children score lower on these tests because they were genetically inferior or because their conditions of life had not prepared them for the kinds of knowledge being tested? White Americans generally opted for the former explanation, while black social scientists—including E. Franklin Frazier, Charles S. Johnson, Howard H. Long, and Horace Mann Bond—fervently argued for a cultural interpretation. Unfortunately, it took more than forty years for the essential humanity of their views to be even grudgingly included in the national agenda, and remnants of the genetic inferiority argument are still prevalent today.[20]

From the 1930s, when the disparities between black and white educational opportunities in the South were at their widest, to the early 1960s, when the civil rights movement blossomed, the central story in black educational history has been the legal strategy that culminated in the *Brown* decision. Because the U.S. Supreme Court had maintained in *Plessy v. Ferguson* in 1896 that separate but equal was the law of the land, this strategy had two stages: first, to go after the inequities at graduate and professional schools, highlighting the fact that separate was *not* equal; and second, to attack segregation itself at the public school level.[21]

A group of lawyers, many associated with the Howard University Law School and the NAACP, slowly but surely built a foundation of legal precedents establishing that equal education required more than access to a few books—that it also depended on the quality of in-school associations. Black psychologists and other social scientists aided the cause through studies showing that segregation was mentally oppressive to all. Finally, in 1954, the nine justices of the Supreme Court, in a unanimous opinion, asked, "Does segregation of children in public schools solely on the basis of race, even though the physical facilities and other 'tangible' factors may be equal, deprive the children of the minority group of equal educational opportunities?" Their answer was straightforward: "We believe that it does. . . . We conclude that in the field of public education the doctrine of 'separate but equal' has no place." The rocky road to the proper education of black children was certainly not completed with this decision, and many formidable barriers remained, but at least de jure segregation was no longer a constitutionally approved detour.[22]

What lessons should we learn from this historical recapitulation? One is certainly that black people have shown a persistent commitment to schooling, as demonstrated by their struggle and sacrifice. Even under the most trying circumstances black communities have energetically organized their social resources and political will to improve the education of their children. Committed student-teacher relationships and the dedication of black educators who

Even under the most trying circumstances black communities have energetically organized their social resources and political will to improve the education of their children.

11

strove against the odds created an infrastructure for black intellectual advancement. Another lesson is that the concept of education the black community has implicitly adopted—education for liberation, for citizenship, for personal and collective power and advancement—has deep roots. While the contemporary perspective on schooling is narrow and utilitarian, the black perspective has long been rich and inclusive. This view of education cannot avoid moral training and social and political commitment. It includes mastery of basic skills and proficiencies, but it recognizes, as well, the multiple intelligences that need to be developed in a truly educated person.

Finally, we must not forget the negative and counterproductive lessons of our past: "Why try?" the young scholar asked in 1819, and many of our children ask the same haunting question today. "Why try?" is the other side of the history of the continual struggles black Americans have faced.[23]

America is moving backward—not forward—in its
efforts to achieve the full participation of minority
citizens in the life and prosperity of the nation. . . .
If we allow these disparities to continue, the United
States inevitably will suffer a compromised quality
of life and a lower standard of living. . . . In brief, we
will find ourselves unable to fulfill the promise of the
American dream.

—Commission on Minority Participation
in Education and American Life, 1988

Barriers to Successful Schooling

Despite the social and political accomplishments of
blacks since the *Brown* decision, formidable barriers
still diminish the education of many black children
and adolescents. These obstacles include lingering
"rumors of inferiority," as some have called the
psychological dimensions of the problem, as well as
bureaucratic and classroom practices that deny black
children the necessary resources and opportunities to
fulfill their potential.[24] This discriminatory treatment
takes many forms. As a task force from Champaign,
Illinois, told the Board of Inquiry for the National
Coalition of Advocates for Children, the education of
black children is circumscribed by:

> . . . their virtual noninvolvement in school activities;
> underrepresentation in programs for the gifted and
> overrepresentation in special education; disproportionate
> discipline referrals, resulting in suspension and expul-
> sion; interactions with some staff members who do not
> know or exhibit appreciation of values inherent in black
> culture; interactions with many staff members who
> communicate low expectations for their behavior and
> achievement; and the destruction of hopes that comes
> from living in a community in which black unemploy-
> ment is high and a general feeling exists that adult
> opportunities for success are limited.[25]

Supporting data bear out this damning assessment:

Despite the social and political accomplishments of blacks since the Brown *decision, formidable barriers still diminish the education of many black children and adolescents.*

- In 1980, black children were three times more likely than white children to be placed in classes for the educable mentally retarded, and only one-half as likely to be in classes for the gifted and talented.

- In high schools, black students are suspended about three times more often than white students.

- Although black students make up slightly more than 16 percent of the nation's elementary and secondary public school enrollments, only seven to eight percent of public school teachers are black.

- Since 1965, the unemployment rates for black men and black women have increased in virtually all age categories between 18 and 64 years old.[26]

Nevertheless, some gains have been made: black students' scores on the Scholastic Aptitude Test (SAT) have increased moderately, and during the 1970s, black 9- and 13-year-olds showed strong improvements in reading and math scores, particularly in the southeastern states. On the whole, black high school completion rates have improved in recent years. If incremental gains like these can be made, a wholesale effort could break through the remaining failures. Yet black college enrollment has declined dramatically since the mid-1970s (falling from 50 percent of recent high school graduates in 1977 to 36.5 percent in 1986), and in some central city schools black dropout rates are intolerably high, approaching and sometimes exceeding 50 percent. At the high school level, black students are greatly overrepresented in vocational tracks and underrepresented in academic programs.[27]

The New World Foundation has characterized current educational conditions as "a crisis of inequality." "School failure for lower income and minority students," the report charges, "has reached epidemic proportions. . . . The taproot of this failure is the chronic inequality in the school resources allocated to poor and declining communities, in the ways that learning is stratified and structured, in the ways that schools treat diverse needs and potentials." The result, this study notes, is "second-class schooling."[28]

The barriers to black educational achievement begin with the economic and social status of the black population. As is well-known and amply documented, schools often reinforce social inequalities rather than overcome them, and the perceived life chances of low-income students have been shown to inhibit their scholastic motivation.[29] Since vast segments of the black community in the 1980s suffer from a pervasive and widening economic depression characterized by a sharp decline in real income, high unemployment rates, a steep increase in the proportion of single-parent families, and a feminization of poverty, it is hardly surprising that students come to school with depressed expectations.[30]

These social phenomena influence patterns of schooling and educational attainment in a variety of ways. They are likely to lead to early parenting, with some 50 percent of teenage mothers failing to graduate from high school. Teen fathers are 40 percent less likely to graduate than their nonparenting peers. In addition, the likelihood of graduation for both black males and females is closely linked to their mother's level of education.[31]

Children from poor families are three to four times more likely to forgo completing high school than those from more affluent families. (When family income is statistically controlled, black and white dropout rates are remarkably similar; interestingly enough, poor blacks have a slightly lower dropout rate than poor whites, 24.6 percent to 27.1 percent, respectively.)[32]

In the context of changes in the U.S. economy, the dropout problem among black youth is all the more devastating. In urban centers over the past two decades, job losses have been heaviest in fields that require less than a high school education, and job growth has been greatest in fields requiring at least some post-secondary education. Broadly speaking, cities have been changing from centers of goods processing and distribution to centers of information processing and higher-order service administration. In New York City, for example, jobs requiring lower educational attainments decreased by 492,000 between 1970 and 1984, while those requiring higher educational attainments increased by 239,000. In

Schools often reinforce social inequalities rather than overcome them.

15

Philadelphia, during the same period there were 172,000 fewer jobs for those with less than a high school education, and 39,000 more for those with some higher education; in Atlanta, 9,000 lower-level jobs were lost, while 37,000 higher-level jobs were opened. Although increases in certain categories of jobs are occurring nationwide—including secretaries, bookkeepers, retail sales workers, nurses' aides, cooks and chefs, cashiers, and so on—these jobs typically require at least a high school diploma and are often far removed from the central city areas where growing numbers of low-income, poorly educated minorities reside.[33]

Surprisingly, for blacks, unlike whites, each additional year of schooling beyond the elementary level does not result in commensurate gains in employability. In fact, in 1982, black men and women who graduated from high school actually had slightly higher unemployment rates than those who completed only one to three years of high school. Only with the attainment of a college degree does schooling beyond the elementary years make a substantial difference in black employment patterns.[34]

The dampened hopes of many black children often smolder in lingering resentments manifested in drug and alcohol abuse; passivity, apathy, and noninvolvement in school work; and inappropriate classroom behaviors. Certainly, discontinuities between school and community are not unique to the black experience. The social alienation among American youth in general, indicated by the extensive use of drugs and alcohol, to take one example, represents a national crisis. But the combined effects of these social conditions place black youth at a particularly severe disadvantage, and the educational institutions of our society have failed to respond effectively.[35]

One indisputable way in which schools institutionalize social inequalities is through the gross stereotyping of black children. Mistaken notions about low-income people and their lifestyles form the basis for low expectations and self-fulfilling prophesies of failure in school. Research has revealed that teachers form negative, inaccurate, and inflexible expectations based on such attributes as the race and perceived social class of their pupils. These expectations result

Mistaken notions about low-income people and their lifestyles form the basis for low expectations and self-fulfilling prophesies of failure in school.

16

in different treatment of minority and white students and affect the minority students' self-concept, academic motivation, and level of aspiration as they conform, over time, more and more closely to what is expected of them.

Our concern is not with expectations per se; as observant parents and responsible educators well know, reasonable and logical inferences concerning pupil performance can be extremely helpful in determining learning goals and setting levels of instruction. Rather, the issue is the accuracy of expectations and especially the ability of educators to revise their expectations in light of new information on student progress. When teachers perceive a black child as a "low achiever" and regard this condition as permanent and unchangeable, the child is not likely to succeed. Moreover, as Eleanor Leacock notes in *Teaching and Learning in City Schools,* the apathy and lack of motivation that teachers decry in urban classrooms "is all too readily ascribed to lack of interest in learning derived from home backgrounds. In fact, however, this lack of interest and response can be seen as children returning to their teachers exactly what they have been receiving from them."[36]

When teachers perceive a black child as a "low achiever" and regard this condition as permanent and unchangeable, the child is not likely to succeed.

Any discussion of low expectations for black and other minority youth must face the issue of tracking, i.e., ability grouping. Many teachers, administrators, and even parents defend tracking on several grounds—that the academic needs of students are better served through homogeneous groupings, that less-capable students do not suffer emotional stress from competition with their brighter classmates, that teaching is easier. The research literature, however, reveals strikingly little evidence supporting any of these claims. Rather, study after study indicates: (1) that black and minority students are disproportionately placed in the lower-ability, non-college-bound tracks; (2) that the net effect of tracking is to exaggerate the initial differences among students rather than to provide the means to better accommodate them; and (3) that tracking results in an altered "opportunity structure" detrimental to those in the bottom tracks, because the nature and content of their instruction is systematically different from that of other students. In this regard, students placed in the

17

Black and other low-income students are often imprisoned in the bottom tracks, shunted away from mainstream classroom instruction.

low tracks have been shown to have less access to resources (including, in some cases, the school's best teachers); less instruction in higher-order thinking skills, with more emphasis placed on rote training and workbook lessons; and, overall, less time set aside for review of homework and other academic activities, with a greater stress on matters of mindless procedure and strict discipline.[37]

The inflexibility of track placements, like the rigidity of teacher expectations, represents a problem of paramount proportions. Black and other low-income students are often imprisoned in the bottom tracks, shunted away from mainstream classroom instruction. In fact, this is one of the major reasons that many black students fall further and further behind their peers academically as they advance through the grades. Even most proponents of tracking agree that students should be able to move up the academic hierarchy as their abilities dictate. Yet, most frequently, black students are dropped into low-ability groups, sometimes at a very early age, with little possibility of movement upward. James Rosenbaum, in *Making Inequality,* likens inflexible tracking to a sports tournament: "When you win, you win only the right to go on to the next round; when you lose, you lose forever."[38]

Along with tracking, standardized testing has been one of the most controversial educational topics of the past quarter century. Opponents charge, among other things, that the tests discriminate against minorities, while proponents support their use for credentialing, track assignments, and other purposes. Spurred by the excellence movement, state legislatures over the past few years have increasingly mandated testing for promotions and as a measure to determine public accountability. The debate continues unabated. In many ways we agree with the assessment offered in a report by the New World Foundation:

> Testing itself is not the core issue. The issues are whether the test used is valid for what it purports to measure; whether the test assesses performance or dictates performance; whether the results are used to correct institutional deficiencies or to stratify students. By these criteria, we have ample reason to challenge the

extraordinary legitimacy now vested in standardized
testing and competitive test scores.[39]

Thoughtful critics of standardized testing have raised
a number of concerns in addition to the issue of
cultural bias, including: (1) that many tests classify
students according to statistical procedures based on a
bell-shaped curve, thus providing a rank order but not
necessarily indicating the level of mastery that has
been achieved; (2) that there is more to schooling and
learning than simply how well students perform on
time-restricted, multiple-choice tests and that a wide
range of abilities and proficiencies are not tapped by
these measures; (3) that the tests are typically used
not as diagnostic tools for effective teaching and
remediation but as punitive measures for labeling,
tracking, promotion, and so on; and (4) that over-
emphasis upon standardized testing subverts true education, undermining the curriculum and eroding the
quality of teaching.[40]

Overall, then, serious questions must be raised about
the validity of standardized testing and its effects not
only upon black and minority children but upon
quality education for all. We advocate the development and sensitive use of a variety of methods for
assessing both school and student performance.
Standardized tests do have their place, particularly as
research tools in comparative assessments of groups
of students across classrooms and school districts and
as criteria for public accountability (under strict
guidelines for interpretation). But, we believe, to
assess individual performance in order to decide on a
student's academic program, a variety of measures
must be employed. Contrary to the long-standing
view that intelligence is a unitary phenomenon
measurable by a single test, we believe—and recent
research confirms—that all people are blessed with
multiple intelligences, which can be tapped through a
variety of teaching methods. Only as schools expand
their vision of individual capacities and abilities will
education become truly inclusive.[41]

Expanded concepts of intelligence go hand in hand
with a broader view of the curriculum and an increased minority presence within the teaching force.
Lip-service is often paid to the goal of multicultural
education, yet it is frequently neglected as an across-

> *We believe—and
> recent research
> confirms—that all
> people are blessed
> with "multiple intelli-
> gences," which can be
> tapped through a
> variety of teaching
> methods.*

the-board curricular concern; when implemented, it is often isolated as an ethnic event or adventure. We do not argue for "relevance" as a reduction in curricular standards, as some opponents have charged; nor is our goal the inclusion of rap music in auditorium performances (although, as a means of teaching poetry and creative expression, "rap" and other black art forms might indeed be employed). We do believe that our schools must reflect and creatively utilize the pluralistic nature of our society to enhance the educational endeavor.[42]

Rather than increasing their presence in the schools, black teachers are becoming an endangered species, dropping to as little as five percent of the teaching force at a time when black student enrollments are increasing. Many reasons have been given for the declining number of black instructors, ranging from the increased use of standardized examinations of teachers to expanded opportunities for blacks and other minorities, especially women, in other professions. Surely a mix of these factors is involved. Current efforts to transform teaching from an occupation into a respected profession can play a critical role in rectifying this problem. Career ladders that freed teachers from performing the same tasks year after year might attract and retain ambitious, talented blacks as well as whites to the profession. Likewise, recruitment programs and other incentives can be improved. Our point is twofold: first, the reform of the teaching profession is a potentially important component in enhancing the achievement of black youth; and, second, increasing the number of black educators must be a central aspect of this reform drive.

*R*ather than increasing their presence in the schools, black teachers are becoming an "endangered species."

Teachers can spark a spirit of inquiry in students only when they themselves feel a spirit of inquiry and development. Yet the burgeoning literature on teacher burnout vividly depicts the isolation, redundancy, and stress in many teachers' lives. Schools need to provide collaborative environments that support the intellectual development of teachers as well as students. They need to encourage creativity and risk-taking, challenging teachers to broaden their pedagogical repertoires and students to become academically engaged. Both black teachers and black students are alienated from the schools when the structure and the content of education is trivialized.[43]

Finally, one critical barrier to school success is the lack of early childhood education programs. Research findings consistently and unequivocally indicate that the Head Start and Chapter 1 (formerly Title 1) entitlement programs not only benefit low-income children but are a sound social investment as well. For every dollar paid for Head Start, it has been estimated that we save seven dollars in related social service costs, and an investment of $600 for a child for one year of Chapter 1 services can save $4,000 in costs for repeating a grade. Yet neither program has ever adequately served all who are eligible. Head Start, the most successful of the 1960s initiatives, reaches only 16 to 18 percent of the 2.5 million eligible children.

Head Start and Title 1 entitlement programs not only benefit low-income children but are a sound social investment as well.

When the Reagan administration reorganized Chapter 1 in 1981, the program was severely watered down. In 1985, only about 54 percent of the children eligible for Chapter 1 received the compensatory services to which they were entitled, down from 75 percent in 1980, and funding decreased by approximately 29 percent between 1979 and 1985. Mandates for parental participation were callously and arbitrarily weakened; several states were allowed to eliminate certain academic and preschool components; and, according to Children's Defense Fund estimates, approximately 900,000 potential recipients lost services. Failure to support these programs represents a criminally negligent social policy.[44]

The effects of poverty, unemployment, racism, funding cutbacks, and the general conditions of life in poor communities seep into the schools in myriad ways. While we do not expect schools in and of themselves to solve the social woes of American society, neither will we tolerate their continued compliance in deflating the aspirations of black youth. The 1966 Coleman Report has been justly criticized, but one point raised by that study is appropriate in this regard: "equality of educational opportunity through schools must imply a strong effect of schools that is independent of the child's immediate social environment, and that strong independent effect is not present in American

21

schools."[45] Until educational institutions accomplish this paramount task of overcoming social obstacles rather than recreating and reinforcing them, equality of educational opportunity for black children will elude us.

The search should be for "good enough" schools—
not meant to imply minimal standards of talent and
competence, but rather to suggest a view that wel-
comes change and anticipates imperfection. . . . I am
not arguing for lower standards or reduced quality. I
am urging a definition of good schools that sees them
as whole, changing, and imperfect. It is in articulat-
ing and confronting each of these dimensions that one
moves closer and closer to the institutional supports
of good education.

—Sara Lawrence Lightfoot, 1983

Improving Schools
for Black Children

By the late 1960s and early 1970s, the public
policy debate over the education of black children,
particularly in urban areas, took on a decidedly
pessimistic tone. Bureaucratic maneuvering thwarted
community control activists, while the ideals of the
1960s' social programs were submerged by a wave of
academic studies questioning the gains that had been
won. The early evaluations of Head Start, Title 1,
and other compensatory education programs did not
demonstrate the quick spurts in IQ scores that many
had hoped for—though neither problems in implementation and funding nor the narrow conceptions of
achievement that marred some early efforts were
prominently examined. The failure to create an
immediate "educational renaissance" was hastily
explained through resurrected notions of black
genetic inferiority. Moreover, popular interpretations
of two influential research reports, John Coleman's
Equality of Educational Opportunity (1966) and
Christopher Jencks' *Inequality* (1972), fostered a
public sentiment summed up in the catch-phrase
"Schools don't work." To the extent that these
studies and others stressed family background as the
determining factor in children's school achievements,

their results were generally taken to mean that the poor showing in school among black and minority youth had little to do with the schools themselves. For people who were predisposed to a view of black cultural and academic inferiority, it was easy to interpret the message: It's not the schools' fault, it's the kids'! Schools were off the hook.[46]

It was easy to interpret the message: it's not the schools' fault, it's the kids'!

In response to this gloomy climate of opinion regarding the education of black children, Ron Edmonds and others launched the effective schools movement. They sought to promote the social equity concerns of black and low-income children by demonstrating the existence and determining the characteristics of effective urban schools.

Subsequent research has identified five central characteristics of schools that successfully educate students: (1) strong administrative leadership, especially a principal and a core group of teachers who serve to bring together a consensus around school goals and purposes; (2) a positive climate of expectations that embraces all children; (3) an orderly and disciplined school atmosphere conducive to the academic tasks at hand; (4) a clear focus on pupils' acquisition of skills and knowledge as the fundamental school objective; and (5) frequent monitoring and assessment of pupil performance.[47]

The effective schools literature of the last 10 to 15 years has also influenced other conceptions of school improvement. Mastery learning programs are an example of a recent initiative that considers the vast majority of students educable and fosters the view that it is the school's responsibility to serve all comers. These programs are grounded in the belief that 80 to 90 percent of all children can learn material if it follows a clear, logical sequence, if the students receive systematic rewards and reinforcement, and if the teaching strategies are designed to match the context. Black and poor children can learn, this set of studies indicate, when schools and society agree to ensure that they do so.[48]

The research literature on school improvement has also been deepened and enriched in recent years by analyses of the School Development Program initiated at the Yale Child Study Center by James Comer.

Working with the New Haven Public Schools, Comer and his colleagues have focused on enhancing the social context for teaching and learning school by school, particularly by improving relationships among staff, students, and parents.[49]

Comer notes that the social distance between schools and the communities they serve has changed significantly over the past generation. We can no longer assume that parents and teachers share values, and in any case, children are exposed to a great range of information and conflicting views by television, videos, radio, and other sources as they attempt to make sense of their world. But Comer does not view the past nostalgically. He recognizes that schooling must change with the times. It is not enough to raise standards arbitrarily; we must also construct new patterns of interactions so that the powerful social networks that nurture and develop the child in the home and community are less alienated from the culture of the school. Too often, black parents are called upon by the school only for disciplinary troubles, or when their child has an academic problem. The process of building supportive relationships for black children, of creating a true learning community that respects diversity of cultures, languages, and learning styles just as it nurtures the life of the mind, naturally includes parents in substantive educational matters.

For although the society has grown increasingly complex, young children are no more innately intelligent or socially developed than they ever have been. They still need consistent relationships with supportive adults to help them mediate their experiences and thus to learn how to understand and to control the world around them. As Comer explains:

> It is the attachment and identification with a meaningful adult that motivates or reinforces a child's desire to turn the nonsense sounds and syllables we call the alphabet, to letters, words, and sentences (and accomplish many other school tasks) *before* they have obvious meaning and benefit. But once done, such achievement is inherently rewarding. This gives a school setting greater value and, in turn, increases the likelihood of student acceptance of the attitudes, expectations, and ways of the school. Thus, the ability of the staff to permit and

James Comer and his colleagues have focused on enhancing the social context for teaching and learning school by school, particularly by improving relationships among staff, students, and parents.

25

promote attachment and identification with them is critical to learning.[50]

Yet, for a variety of reasons such supportive relationships between care givers and children frequently do not develop; instead, conflicts develop based upon class, race, income, or culture, and the skills and abilities that many children learn as useful outside of school do not help them achieve academic success. Mounting accusations and aggression then start to spiral out of control; children begin to respond to this negatively charged situation by acting out their rejection of the norms and values of the school, by losing confidence, or by inwardly withdrawing from a confrontation they sense they cannot win. Teachers and staff, in turn, see their attitudes and expectations confirmed and justified. As Eleanor Leacock notes:

> Deviations themselves are patterned, and supposedly deviant roles, such as not learning, can become widespread, institutionalized, and as intrinsic to the social structure as supposedly dominant norms. Most nonconforming behavior does not follow from a lack of ability to adjust, but is built into the system as integrally as "acceptable" behavior.[51]

Within this framework, the model of school intervention offered by the School Development Program has several key components. One is the creation of a "no-fault atmosphere," in which blaming and finger-pointing take a back seat to open discussions among administrators, staff, and parents around school and student needs. No single group is assumed to be at fault, and no single initiative, taken by itself, is seen as making a difference. The focus is on creating an interactive social and academic climate that makes the school a desirable place to be, to work, and to learn. The intervention program recognizes that just as teaching and learning are not mechanical processes, relationships supporting cooperation, nurturance, development, and achievement cannot be mandated. Thus, collaborative teams for governance, management, and mental health are created to energize the entire school. These teams, which include administrative leaders, teachers, parents, and specialists in child and adolescent development, work to create networks of communication in order to overcome the departmentalization and hierarchical

We must construct new patterns of interactions so that the powerful social networks that nurture and develop the child in the home and community are less alienated from the culture of the school.

26

fragmentation that turn schools into impersonal bureaucracies.

Parent participation is an essential element in this intervention, although it is difficult to achieve. Distrust often runs high between families and the schools that serve low-income and minority children, with charges and countercharges sending a mixed message to our youth: school is hope; school is the enemy. Yet the New Haven experience has demonstrated that when parents participate in the schools in meaningful, well-conceived, and structured ways, they come to identify with the school's academic concerns. Parents checking homework, working as classroom assistants, volunteering as coordinators of after-school activities, and participating as members of the governance and management teams give black students immediately recognizable adult models. Teachers and parents are seen as being in alliance, working for and believing in common intellectual and social goals. Parents also begin to develop a sense of ownership of the school and feelings of responsibility for academic success. Educational aspirations expand and begin to spread from students to their families as parents decide to reinvest in their own educations.

There are no "quick-fix" solutions or "Band-Aid" remedies which can be applied across the board.

Both the effective schools literature and the school development intervention model have shown that there are no quick-fix solutions or Band-Aid remedies which can be applied across the board. Consensus on educational purposes, a commitment to common goals, and a climate of expectations cannot be imposed on schools from without. Rather, they must come from the collaboration of active participants in the educational process. Thus, a common theme of these and other reform efforts has been reform at the building level—that is, within individual schools.

One promising trend in this regard has been the development of the role of the teacher as researcher, in which classroom instructors systematically attempt to close the cultural gaps separating school from community—investigating, for example, the ways in which differences between speaking styles in the local black community and styles used in classroom discussion might be bridged. Studies since the 1960s have revealed that black English possesses a gram-

27

mar, a system of deep cultural meanings, and a linguistic integrity on a par with that of standard English. Unfortunately, educators had not until recently found a way to bridge the gap between these two language forms in the classroom. Over the last few years, however, researchers such as Shirley Brice Heath have urged parents and teachers to work more closely together to clarify the perplexing discontinuities and thus improve their students' school performance.

The results have been instructive. Teachers have been energized by their new and challenging role and have experimented with different types of question-asking and prereading activities, building upon and expanding the language competencies their students bring to school. Parents are seen as having valuable information that can make a difference in their children's learning. And black children perceive a greater continuity between home and school: their observations and answers no longer constantly corrected before they can complete an idea, they do not feel disparaged. They learn to identify the contexts in which different styles are appropriate, and they improve the language skills necessary for school success.[52]

Again, we are not naive about the complex processes that successfully improve schools. Surmounting the institutionalized patterns of beliefs and behaviors that have, on the whole, thwarted the education of black youth requires a collaborative, evolutionary perspective. As Sara Lawrence Lightfoot notes in her book, *The Good High School,* "institutional invigoration and restoration is a slow, cumbersome process. . . . there are jagged stages of institutional development . . . . [and a] staged quality of goodness."

The black community must not wait for the educational millennium. It must make conscious efforts to achieve change through the empowerment of parents, teachers, and students.

The black community must not wait for the educational millennium. It must make conscious efforts to achieve change through the empowerment of parents, teachers, and students. And, as Edmonds stated with regard to the effective schools drive, "if you generally seek the means to educational equity for all our people, you must encourage parents' attention to politics as the greatest instrument of institutional reform extant."[53] Comer agrees:

> Black community organizations—church, fraternal, social and others—must find a way to set expectations and support the development of our children at home and at school. That is precisely what happened when we were largely located in the small towns and rural areas of the South, and in segregated schools. Much has been gained through racial integration in all institutions. And while many White teachers are supportive, the broad-based Black community support for achievement inside and outside schools has been lost and must be restored in some systematic way. . . . As a community we can't abandon the public schools or support public policy that allows the society to do so.[54]

Schools embody the bad as well as the good of society. But we will no longer accept that appraisal as an excuse for failure.

Thus, we call for collective action to improve schooling for black children. Neither cynicism, nor despair, nor undue optimism is appropriate; all of these are comfortable indulgences that militate against constructive educational change. We do not deny that schools embody the bad as well as the good of society. But we will no longer accept that appraisal as an excuse for failure. We must all search for the common ground on which to build an academic foundation for this generation of black youngsters.

The citizens of tomorrow must be equipped as best we know how to equip them, with the techniques which will soften, if not entirely alleviate, the shock of our continuous transition.

—Horace Mann Bond, 1933

Conclusions and Recommendations

We began this appraisal of the black educational experience by asserting the capacity of black children to master their schoolwork and by calling upon the black community to mobilize its considerable social and political resources to achieve equal educational opportunity for all. In fact, it is our belief in the academic and human potential of black youth that makes the current levels of underachievement intolerable. Our basic goal must be to raise the perceived ceiling on black talent.

Another, equally important purpose of this defense of black intellectual capacity is to combat the rampant "caste spirit" that W. E. B. Du Bois referred to in 1912 and which still today circumscribes black life. The undereducation of black children does not exist in a void; the school is not an isolated social institution. The crisis in education is also a crisis in democratic citizenship. We have already discussed both the transformations taking place in the American economy and the proposals for school reform that promote a narrow view of "excellence" devoid of social justice concerns for black youth and their families. If these distorted reforms are implemented without input from the black community, it is clearly in danger of being locked out of the new economic arrangements that will structure U.S. society well into the 21st century. We must respond forcefully to the myopic perceptions that perpetuate the black underclass.

31

Our recommendations for progressive educational reform fall into three categories:

- recognizing the centrality of human relationships;

- eliminating barriers to effective teaching and learning;

- mobilizing physical and political resources.

Recognizing the Centrality of Human Relationships

Black parents must become actively involved in the educational process, and schools must welcome their participation.

Schools have primary responsibility for the education of our children, but that does not absolve us of our own obligation to ensure that the schools are working. We cannot allow educators to blame black children and their families for the underachievement and apathy so prevalent in many urban school systems. Reaching consensus around academic goals and purposes must be seen as the starting point in developing positive relationships among all of the central actors in the educational scene—teachers, students, administrators, and parents. The black community must also get involved in this process through political activism at the grassroots level. Only a united front can become an effective agent for educational achievement by black youth.

Schools must become less impersonal.

It is extraordinarily difficult for children to become engaged in their lessons, or for teachers to establish productive relationships with their students, in school buildings that resemble large factories. Yet, when Roxbury High School in Boston was about to be closed down in the early 1980s, for example, black students' worries about being "lost," "unnoticed," and "overlooked" in their new school were cavalierly dismissed by central office authorities. But such concerns are very real for all adolescents, particularly those whose race has been treated as invisible and who throughout their lives have experienced large

Reaching consensus around academic goals must be seen as the starting point in developing positive relationships among central actors in the educational scene—teachers, students, administrators, and parents.

32

doses of neglect and indifference. The successes of the School Development Program in New Haven, on the other hand, along with certain alternative efforts such as the Central Park East School in New York, indicate that a sense of identification and connection can make a substantial difference in black children's intellectual development.[55]

The advantages of large schools with a great variety of programs, curricular offerings, laboratories, and technical resources must be balanced against human needs for connection and identification. The house system of organization, already in place in many suburban schools, might be replicated in urban areas so that students not only have a homeroom but also a relatively small network of students and staff with whom they can connect for guidance, support, and friendship. Parents as well as children are more likely to become involved when the school structures are more easily negotiable and less alienating. School spirit should not be confined to those who engage in sports or other extracurricular activities; it should enliven the day-to-day academic affairs of the institution as well.

Schools complain that too much beyond education is expected of them; one way to relieve that burden is for schools to direct parents to sources of help.

Schools must establish closer ties with other social services.

We are advocating not that schools provide a full range of social services for black and low-income students but rather that our educational institutions provide a liaison to social services for parents and children requiring help. Schools are the only institutions in our society in which the acquisition and transmission of skills and knowledge are the primary focus, and we do not want to change this essential mission. But schools are necessarily a focal point for a variety of family problems that undermine this mission.

School-to-work transition programs and school-based health clinics—a topic vigorously debated of late—represent an expanded view of the educational endeavor. Schools must also become knowledgeable of and connected to the communities of the children they serve. A coordinator of social services might be established in the schools to institutionalize this liaison role. The coordinator could direct individuals and families to relevant services at the state, local, and community levels. (In addition to public agencies, nearby churches and other black civic organizations can play an important and well-managed helping role within the black community, providing such services as tutoring, literacy training, housing, and day care.) Beyond academic counseling and guidance—which themselves need repair and increased emphasis—schools can enhance their educational role by facilitating access to the social services needed by students and their families. Schools complain that too much beyond education is expected of them; one way to relieve that burden is systematically to direct parents to sources of help.[56]

Eliminating Barriers to Effective Teaching and Learning

Schools must recruit more black teachers.

Low numbers of black teachers constitute a fundamental barrier to enhanced achievement by black students.[57] All teachers can serve as role models and can develop classroom environments conducive to learning, but what is the "hidden curriculum," what lessons in citizenship and in social relationships do our children learn, when they notice, as they inevitably do, the absence of people like themselves in positions of authority in their schools? Until more children look into the eyes of teachers and see themselves reflected—and until more teachers look into the eyes of children and see themselves reflected— many of those children will feel excluded from the educational enterprise. All educators must be able to perform the basic human act of acceptance and understanding, but undoubtedly it will be easier to achieve when the teachers' lounge is as multicultural as the curriculum and the classroom.

Until more children look into the eyes of teachers and see themselves reflected—and until more teachers look into the eyes of children and see themselves reflected—many of those children will feel excluded from the educational enterprise.

Both within the black community and in American society as a whole, teaching has lost the high status it formerly held. Among blacks, the teaching profession once meant not only secure employment but also an avenue for sharing intellectual attainments and expressing social commitments through "service to the race." The widespread devaluation of teaching has made education a much less attractive career for

34

black college graduates, who historically had been drawn to this occupation.

We believe that teaching can still fulfill the impulse toward service and community commitment, but to attract more black educators to the schools, certain reforms are necessary. Salaries must be raised and opportunities for professional growth and development should be made available. Incentives for teaching in inner-city schools might halt the exodus of teachers from these schools and highlight social concern for the improvement of urban education. Internships for high school students can provide opportunities for talented black youth to get first-hand experience in the classroom while simultaneously providing community service through tutoring and helping their peers with schoolwork. Teaching should not be a fall-back position; it should be a positive option that is attractive because it meshes with certain intellectual and social abilities, because it offers the opportunity to work with youth, and because it holds the possibility of personal growth and advancement.

Develop sensitive and precise testing procedures for the diagnosis of student abilities and needs.

Schools must expand the ways they monitor a pupil's progress. Student performance on time-restricted, multiple-choice, standardized tests does not show innate aptitude, nor does it indicate whether the test-taker is capable of writing an essay or crafting a poem. Indeed, testing becomes a dangerous instrument of social oppression when test results are seen as revealing native abilities uninfluenced by environmental conditions. Furthermore, overreliance on standardized testing distorts the educational process, determining what is taught in the curriculum rather than assessing student acquisition of an independently determined knowledge base.

We do believe that testing can improve education when used as one of several methods of student appraisal. The effective-schools literature has identified the frequent assessment of pupil progress as a key factor in improving instruction. Thus, although we remain concerned about cultural bias and the distorting influence of overtesting, we do not call for

> *Student performance on time-restricted, multiple-choice, standardized tests does not show innate aptitude, nor does it indicate whether the test-taker is capable of writing an essay or crafting a poem.*

35

the abandonment of standardized testing in the schools. Rather, we believe tests must become more sophisticated and sensitive tools for measurement and diagnosis, which will ultimately help our children progress through their course work.

Rigid systems of tracking and ability grouping should be abandoned.

As noted educator John Goodlad has observed, "The decision to track is essentially one of giving up on the problem of human variability in learning. It is a retreat rather than a strategy."

As noted educator John Goodlad has observed, "The decision to track is essentially one of giving up on the problem of human variability in learning. It is a retreat rather than a strategy. The difference in teachers' expectations for high track as contrasted with low track classes . . . is evidence enough of capitulating rather than addressing the admitted complexities of the problem."[58] Moreover, because research findings consistently indicate that inflexible track placements and rigid ability grouping segregate, stigmatize, and deny those in the bottom tracks the same access to quality education those in the upper tracks receive, we believe that these practices should be ended. It is well known that black and other low-income minority students are overrepresented in the lower-ability tracks in our nation's school systems, yet it is frequently overlooked that the differences in the kind of instruction across tracks makes it increasingly difficult for these students ever to climb up the academic hierarchy. In this way, low expectations and mindless bureaucracy crush the potential of thousands of black youth each year and limit their future opportunities. Staff development programs in multicultural education are an example of a readily available avenue that must be seized upon to address issues of diversity within regular classroom settings.

The curriculum must be expanded to reflect the lives and interests of black and other minority children.

Why must we continually fight for the validity of the black experience as a subject of schooling? It takes nothing away from Shakespeare or Emily Dickinson to include the dramas of August Wilson and the poetry of Langston Hughes as an integral part of the school curriculum. All children need to see people like themselves express the timeless concerns of humankind and to be symbolically represented in the classroom as worthy of discourse. "I, too, sing America," Hughes once wrote. A multicultural curriculum is an imperative for a multicultural society; all children will benefit from learning the extraordinary richness of their heterogeneous culture.

All black children must have the opportunity for a quality education.

The goal of the struggle to end segregation has been equal opportunity for quality education for blacks. But although economically successful black parents today can send their children to good desegregated schools, public or private, poor black children still do not have such options. They remain, 34 years after *Brown,* racially isolated, largely segregated, and subjected to inferior schooling. Consequently, we must fight for a decent education for black children wherever they are, whether in desegregated, integrated, or all-black schools.

Mobilizing Physical and Political Resources

Fund Head Start and Chapter 1.

The Children's Defense Fund's FY '89 "Preventative Investment Agenda" notes that in order for Head Start to reach just half of the eligible three-to five-year-old poor children in America, it will have to receive some $400 million in each of the next five years. For Chapter 1 to be extended to all those entitled to receive its services, its funding will have to be increased by $500 million over this same period. While these dollar figures might seem mind-boggling, it is instructive to realize that every year $12.4 billion in revenue is lost because capital gains on inherited corporate stock are not taxed.[59] Moreover, these demonstrably successful programs actually save the country money in the long run.

It takes nothing away from Shakespeare or Emily Dickinson to include the dramas of August Wilson and the poetry of Langston Hughes as an integral part of the school curriculum.

Effective education must lead to effective participation in the economy.

As long as substantial numbers of black youth come to the realistic conclusion, based upon the widespread unemployment around them, that schooling will not

37

pay off in decent job opportunities, their motivation will suffer. Pervasive unemployment undermines those positive messages that do link education, success, and jobs. Moreover, the structural isolation of low-income communities prevents many of our youth from seeing the nature of the jobs performed by their parents and other adult figures. Black children, like all others, can quickly perceive when the rules of the game are stacked against them; when rhetoric fails to jibe with reality. Meaningful employment opportunities, we are convinced, will demonstrate to black children that they have a place in our society and that persistence in school is worthwhile.

Furthermore, survey data that reveal extremely low levels of literacy among black seventeen-year-olds and young adults portend a national tragedy.[60] The productive capacity of the U.S. work force is diminished when large segments of the population do not receive the necessary training to contribute to the well-being of society. The prosperity of the nation depends upon the effective development of human resources even more than on technological improvements.

All segments of the black community must assume a greater responsibility for the education of black youth.

We call upon all black people to apply their skills and abilities aggressively on behalf of our youth. In the past, because of residential segregation and other factors, black Americans from a range of socioeconomic levels interacted daily. In recent years, the black population has itself become polarized. Understandably, many middle- and upper-income blacks have left the inner cities, the public schools, and thus the black communities to which they had belonged.

Middle-class black adults are still needed as positive role models for less fortunate black youth. These adults can work to strengthen community programs that identify and foster black talent. Black historical societies and creative arts groups can expand their outreach efforts; churches might use extra space for supervised tutoring activities; parents might take an extra child or two to the circus or to see a parade. No

Meaningful employment opportunities will demonstrate to black children that they have a place in our society and that persistence in school is worthwhile.

one in the black community can afford to stand on the sidelines.

The improvement of public education must be the principal objective of the black community in the next decade.

We can meet the challenge of ensuring a world-class education for our children only through political activism. All segments of the black community must demand that schools have the staff, policies, and resources necessary to their tasks. Quality education, as described in this essay, can and must be a political issue cutting across race and class and reverberating from neighborhoods to state capitals to the White House.

We can meet the challenge of ensuring a world-class education for our children only through political activism.

39

Notes

Introduction

1. See Stephen S. Baratz and Joan C. Baratz, "Early Childhood Intervention: The Social Science Base of Institutional Racism," *Harvard Educational Review,* Vol. 40, No. 1 (Winter 1970), pp. 31-50; Eleanor B. Leacock (ed.), *The Culture of Poverty: A Critique* (New York: Simon and Schuster, 1971); Caroline Hodges Persell, *Education and Inequality* (New York: The Free Press, 1977).

2. See E. Franklin Frazier, *The Negro Family in the United States* (Chicago: University of Chicago Press, 1939); Kenneth Clark, *Dark Ghetto: Dilemmas of Social Power* (New York: Harper & Row, 1965).

3. See Ronald Edmonds, "A Discussion of the Literature and Issues Related to Effective Schooling," Harvard University, undated, unpublished; James Comer, *School Power* (New York: The Free Press, 1980).

4. Ronald Edmonds, "Effective Schools for the Urban Poor," *Educational Leadership*, Oct. 1979, p. 23.

5. Linda Darling-Hammond, *Equality and Excellence: The Educational Status of Black Americans* (New York: College Entrance Examination Board 1985); Children's Defense Fund, *A Briefing Book on the Status of American Children in 1988* (Washington, DC: 1988).

6. See James Comer, "Is 'Parenting' Essential to Good Teaching?" *NEA Today,* Jan. 1988, pp. 34-40.

7. See Gerald S. Lesser, *Children and Television* (New York: Random House, 1974).

8. See Henry M. Levin, "The Educationally Disadvantaged: A National Crisis," *Public/Private Ventures,* July, 1985; Bastian et al., *Choosing Equality;* Children's Defense Fund, *A Children's Defense Fund Budget* (Washington, DC: 1987).

41

The Historical Context

9. Horace Mann Bond, *The Education of the Negro in the American Social Order* (1934; reprinted New York: Octagon Books, Inc., 1966), pp. 463, 433, 13.

10. Quoted in Leon Litwack, *North of Slavery* (Chicago: University of Chicago Press, 1961), pp. 153-154.

11. See Thomas Webber, *Deep Like the Rivers: Education in the Slave Quarter Community, 1831-1860* (New York: W.W. Norton, 1976); John Boles, *Black Southerners, 1619-1860* (Lexington: University of Kentucky Press, 1984).

12. See Carter G. Woodson, *The Education of the Negro Prior to 1861* (1919; reprinted New York: Arno Press, 1968), pp. 170-171.

13. Litwack, *North of Slavery*, p. 133.

14. See Stanley Schultz, *The Culture Factory* (New York: Oxford University Press, 1973); Litwack, *North of Slavery*.

15. W.E.B. Du Bois, *Black Reconstruction* (New York: 1935), p. 123; Booker T. Washington, *Up from Slavery* (New York: Doubleday, 1906), p. 22.

16. Bond, *The Education of the Negro in the American Social Order*, p. 57.

17. See Rayford Logan, *The Betrayal of the Negro* (New York: Collier Books, 1954); John Hope Franklin, *From Slavery to Freedom*, 4th edition (New York: Alfred A. Knopf, 1974); John Hope Franklin, "Jim Crow Goes to School: The Genesis of Legal Segregation in the South," *South Atlantic Quarterly*, Vol. 43 (Spring 1959).

18. See Bond, *The Education of the Negro;* C. Vann Woodward, *Origins of the New South, 1877-1913* (Baton Rouge: Louisiana State University Press, 1971); Logan, *The Betrayal of the Negro;* George Fredrickson, *The Black Image in the White Mind* (New York: Harper & Row, 1971).

19. For a sample of their differing views, see Booker T. Washington's "Industrial Education for the Negro" and W. E. B. Du Bois' "The Talented Tenth,"

both in Washington et al., *The Negro Problem* (1903; reprinted New York: Arno Press, 1969).

20. See Vincent P. Franklin, "Black Social Scientists and the Mental Testing Movement, 1920-1940," in Reginald Jones (ed.), *Black Psychology* (New York: Harper & Row, 1980); Robert Homel, *Down From Equality: Black Chicagoans and the Public Schools* (Urbana: University of Illinois Press, 1984).

21. See Richard Kluger, *Simple Justice* (New York: Vintage Books, 1975).

22. See text of *Brown* decision in Kluger, *Simple Justice*, pp. 781-782.

23. See Sara Lawrence Lightfoot, *Worlds Apart: Relationships Between Families and Schools* (New York: Basic Books, 1978), pp. 125-175.

Barriers to Successful Schooling

24. See Jeff Howard and Ray Hammond, "Rumors of Inferiority," *The New Republic*, Sept. 9, 1985, pp. 17-21.

25. Quoted in *Barriers to Excellence: Our Children at Risk* (Boston: National Coalition of Advocates for Students, 1985).

26. See *Barriers to Excellence*, p. 10; Darling-Hammond, *Equality and Excellence*, p. 7; *Digest of Educational Statistics, 1985-86* (Washington, DC: Government Printing Office, 1986), pp. 39, 53.

27. Darling-Hammond, *Equality and Excellence;* Children's Defense Fund, *A Briefing Book.*

28. See Ann Bastian et al., *Choosing Equality: The Case for Democratic Schooling* (Philadelphia: Temple University Press, 1986), p. 15.

29. See Lightfoot, *Worlds Apart;* Samuel Bowles and Herbert Gintis, *Schooling in Capitalist America* (New York: Basic Books, 1976); John U. Ogbu, *The Next Generation* (New York: Academic Press, 1974).

30. For an overall perspective on these conditions, see William Julius Wilson, *The Truly Disadvantaged: The Inner City, the Underclass, and Public Policy* (Chicago: University of Chicago Press, 1987).

31. Children's Defense Fund, *Black and White Children in America: Key Facts* (Washington, D.C.: 1985), p. 99; Wilson, *The Truly Disadvantaged,* pp. 28, 61; Michelle Fine, "Why Urban Adolescents Drop Into and Out of Public High School," in Gary Natriello (ed.), *School Dropouts: Patterns and Policies* (New York: Teachers College Press, 1986), pp. 88-105; Children's Defense Fund, *A Briefing Book,* p. 10.

32. Children's Defense Fund, *A Children's Defense Fund Budget, FY 1988* (Washington, DC: 1987), p. 139.

33. Wilson, *The Truly Disadvantaged,* pp. 39-42; *Barriers to Excellence,* pp. 86-89.

34. Darling-Hammond, *Equality and Excellence,* pp. 7-9.

35. See John U. Ogbu, "Cultural Discontinuities and Schooling," *Anthropology and Education Quarterly,* Vol. 13, No. 4, pp. 290-307.

36. Eleanor B. Leacock, *Teaching and Learning in City Schools* (New York: Basic Books, 1969), p. 16. See also Ray C. Rist, "Student Social Class and Teacher Expectations: The Self-fulfilling Prophecy in Ghetto Education," *Harvard Educational Review,* Vol. 40, No. 3 (August 1970), pp. 411-451.

37. See Jeannie Oakes, *Keeping Track: How Schools Structure Inequality* (New Haven: Yale University Press, 1985).

38. James E. Rosenbaum, *Making Inequality* (New York: Wiley-Interscience, 1976), p. 40.

39. Bastian et al., *Choosing Equality,* p. 53.

40. See Asa Hilliard, "Standardization and Cultural Bias Impediments to the Scientific Study and Validation of Intelligence," *Journal of Research and Development in Education,* Vol. 12, No. 2 (Winter 1979), pp. 47-58; *Ability Testing,* Parts 1 and 2 (Washington, D.C.: National Academy Press, 1982).

41. See Howard Gardner, *Frames of Mind: The Theory of Multiple Intelligences* (New York: Basic Books, 1983); Leon J. Kamin, *The Science and Politics of I.Q.* (Potomac, Md: Erlbaum, 1974).

42. See James A. Banks, *Teaching Strategies for Ethnic Studies,* 3rd edition (Boston: Allyn & Bacon, 1984).

43. See Joan C. Baratz, "Black Participation in the Teaching Pool," Paper for the Carnegie Forum's Task Force on Teaching as a Profession, January 1986; Bernard R. Gifford, "Teaching—From Occupation to Profession: The Sine Qua Non of Educational Reform," *New England Journal of Public Policy,* Summer/Fall 1985, pp. 60-75; Bernard R. Gifford, "Prestige and Education: The Missing Link in School Reform," *The Review of Education,* Vol. 10, No. 3 (Summer 1984), pp. 186-198; *Tomorrow's Teachers: A Report of the Holmes Group* (East Lansing, Mich.: Holmes Group, 1986); *A Nation Prepared: Teachers for the 21st Century* (New York: Carnegie Forum on Education and the Economy, 1986).

44. See "The Impact of Head Start on Children, Families and Communities" (Executive Summary), *Final Report of the Head Start Evaluation, Synthesis and Utilization Project* (Washington, D.C.: CSR, Inc., June 1985); Edward Zigler and Jeanette Valentine (eds.), *Project Head Start: A Legacy of the War on Poverty* (New York: The Free Press, 1979); Children's Defense Fund, *A Briefing Book,* p. 8.

45. James S. Coleman et al., *Equality of Educational Opportunity* (Washington, D.C.: Government Printing Office, 1966), p. 325.

Improving Schools for Black Children

46. See Stephen S. Baratz and Joan C. Baratz, "Early Childhood Intervention: The Social Science Base of Institutional Racism," *Harvard Educational Review,* Vol. 40, No. 1 (Winter 1970), pp. 31-50; Arthur R. Jensen, "How Much Can We Boost IQ and Scholastic Achievement," *Harvard Educational Review,* Vol. 39, No. 1 (Winter 1969), pp. 1-123; Coleman et al., *Equality of Educational Opportunity;* Christopher Jencks, *Inequality: A Reassessment of the Effect of Family and Schooling in America* (New York: Harper & Row, 1972); Ronald Edmonds et al., "A Black Response to Christopher Jencks's *Inequality* and Certain Other Issues," in *Perspectives on Inequality,*

Harvard Educational Review Reprint Services No. 8, 1973.

47. Ronald Edmonds, "Effective Schools for the Urban Poor," *Educational Leadership,* October 1979; Edmonds, "A Discussion of the Literature and Issues Related to Effective Schooling"; Daniel U. Levine, Rayna R. Levine, and Eugene E. Eubanks, "Successful Implementation of Instruction at Inner-City Schools," *Journal of Negro Education,* Vol. 54, No. 3 (1985), pp. 313-332; Michael Rutter et al., *15,000 Hours: Secondary Schools and Their Effects on Children* (Cambridge: Harvard University Press, 1979).

48. See Benjamin S. Bloom, *All Our Children Learning: A Primer for Parents, Teachers, and Other Educators* (New York: McGraw-Hill, 1980); Benjamin S. Bloom, "The Search for Methods of Group Instruction as Effective as One-to-One Tutoring," *Educational Leadership,* May 1984, pp. 4-17.

49. The following discussion is drawn from: James Comer's *School Power: Implications of an Intervention Project* (New York: The Free Press, 1980); "Empowering Black Children's Educational Environments," in Harriette Pipes McAdoo and John Lewis McAdoo (eds.), *Black Children: Social, Educational, and Parental Environments* (Beverly Hills: Sage, 1985); "Is 'Parenting' Essential to Good Teaching?" pp. 34-40; "Home-School Relationships as They Affect the Academic Success of Children, *Education and Urban Society,* Vol. 16, No. 3 (May 1984), pp. 323-337; "Parent Participation in the Schools," *Phi Delta Kappan,* Vol. 67, No. 6 (Feb. 1986), pp. 442-446; "Education is the Way Out and Up," *Ebony,* August 1987, pp. 61-66.

50. Comer, "Home-School Relationships," p. 327.

51. Eleanor B. Leacock, *Teaching and Learning in City Schools,* p. 17.

52. See Shirley Brice Heath, *Ways with Words* (New York: Cambridge University Press, 1983); J.L. Dillard, *Black English* (New York: Vintage Books, 1972); Geneva Smitherman, "'What Go Round Come

Round': *King* in Perspective," *Harvard Educational Review*, Vol. 51, No. 1 (February 1981), pp. 40-56.

53. Ron Edmonds, "Effective Schools for the Urban Poor," *Educational Leadership*, Oct. 1979, p. 23.

54. Comer, "Education is the Way Out and Up," p. 66.

Conclusions and Recommendations

55. Deborah Meier, "Central Park East: An Alternative Story," *Phi Delta Kappan*, Vol. 68, No. 10 (June 1987), pp. 753-757.

56. See *Barriers to Excellence*, pp. 55-58.

57. See, for example, Baratz, "Black Participation in the Teaching Pool"; Patricia Albjerg Graham, "Black Teachers: A Drastically Scarce Resource," *Phi Delta Kappan*, April 1987, pp. 598-605.

58. John I. Goodlad, *A Place called School* (New York: McGraw-Hill, 1984), p.297.

59. Children's Defense Fund, *A Briefing Book on the Status of American Children in 1988,* pp. v-vi.

60. National Assessment of Educational Progress, *Literacy: Profiles of America's Young Adults* (Princeton: Educational Testing Service, 1986), p. 39.

The Committee on Policy for Racial Justice

Chairman
Dr. John Hope Franklin
James B. Duke Professor Emeritus
Duke University
Durham, North Carolina

Dr. Bernard E. Anderson
Managing Partner
The Urban Affairs Partnership
Philadelphia, Pennsylvania

Derrick Bell, Esq.
Professor of Law
Harvard Law School
Cambridge, Massachusetts

Mary Frances Berry, Esq.
Geraldine R. Segal Professor of
  American Social Thought
  and History
University of Pennsylvania
Philadelphia, Pennsylvania

Dr. Haywood Burns
Dean, Law School
City University of New York
New York, New York

Lisle C. Carter, Jr., Esq.
General Counsel
United Way of America
Alexandria, Virginia

Dr. Jewel Plummer Cobb
President
California State University
Fullerton, California

Dr. James P. Comer
Maurice Falk Professor of
  Child Psychiatry
Yale University Child Study Center
New Haven, Connecticut

Drew S. Days III, Esq.
Professor of Law
Yale University School of Law
New Haven, Connecticut

Marian Wright Edelman
President
Children's Defense Fund
Washington, D.C.

Christopher Edley, Jr., Esq.
Professor of Law
Harvard Law School
Cambridge, Massachusetts

Dr. James Lowell Gibbs, Jr.
Chair
Department of Anthropology
Stanford University
Stanford, California

Dr. Bernard R. Gifford
Vice President of Education
Apple Computer, Inc.
Cupertino, California

Charles J. Hamilton, Jr., Esq.
Battle, Fowler, Jaffin, Pierce & Kheel
New York, New York

Dr. Matthew Holden, Jr.
Henry L. and Grace M. Doherty
Professor of Government &
  Foreign Affairs
University of Virginia
Charlottesville, Virginia

49

Joyce A. Hughes, Esq.
Professor of Law
Northwestern University School
    of Law
Chicago, Illinois

Dr. Walter J. Leonard
Executive Assistant to the Governor
    & Secretary to the Cabinet
St. Thomas, U.S. Virgin Islands

Sir Arthur Lewis
James S. McDonald Distinguished
    Professor of Economics and
    International Affairs Emeritus
Princeton University
Princeton, New Jersey

Dr. David L. Lewis
Martin Luther King, Jr. Professor
    of History
Rutgers University
New Brunswick, New Jersey

Dr. Sara Lawrence Lightfoot
Professor of Education
Graduate School of Education
Harvard University
Cambridge, Massachusetts

Dr. Milton D. Morris
Director of Research
Joint Center for Political Studies
Washington, D.C.

Eleanor Holmes Norton, Esq.
Professor of Law
Georgetown University Law Center
Washington, D.C.

Dr. William Shack
Professor of Anthropology
University of California
Berkeley, California

Dr. Elliott P. Skinner
Franz Boas Professor of Anthropology
Columbia University
New York, New York

The Honorable Mable Smythe-Haith
Washington, D.C.

Dr. Howard Stanback
Acting Commissioner
Department of Aviation
City of Chicago
Chicago, Illinois

Roger Wilkins, Esq.
Clarence J. Robinson Professor of
    American History and Culture
George Mason University
Fairfax, Virginia

Eddie N. Williams
President
Joint Center for Political Studies
Washington, D.C.

Dr. William J. Wilson
Lucy Flower Distinguished Service
    Professor of Sociology & Public
    Policy
University of Chicago
Chicago, Illinois

_____

Coordinator
Dr. Eleanor Farrar
Vice President
Joint Center for Political Studies
Washington, D.C.

Joint Center for Political Studies
Board of Governors